GONE FAR,
Still Goin'

A BOOK OF POETRY

I0081324

CURTIS ROBBINS, PH.D.

First Edition, 2022

Published by Savory Words Publishing
www.savorywords.com

ISBN 978-1-7377117-4-2
Printed in the United States of America

TABLE OF CONTENTS

AUTHOR'S NOTE

When I started writing poems when I was 14 years old, I began to realize I was playing with words. For many years my experiments with new words meant that many of my poems didn't make any sense. But I kept trying and trying to make the connections. Then one moment, something clicked and the words began to flow and made perfect sense.

My thoughts got deeper and deeper. I started thinking about situations that needed to be written and remembered. On and on I kept writing with pleasure regardless of how good or bad things or situations were. It is with the greatest satisfaction that I share my poems on the following pages. Many of them reflect experiences in my life, such as my Jewish upbringing, my identity development as a Deaf person, and my adventures as a husband, father, professor, and human. All through these years, I happily rewrote, revised, and enjoyed the finalized editions of my works.

Every poem is written for the moment. Every word has a feeling. Every thought has meaning. Thus, every poem goes on—and on. They will always be here for you and me.

*Special thanks to Brian Russell, Pamela Wright,
and Rosa Ramirez.*

Gone Far, Still Goin'

STROKE

A moment was passing
My mind was still
My face was turning
My eyes were spinning
My mouth was drooling
Nothing was certain
I have forgotten the moment

I read the *Washington Post* that morning
Nothing out of the ordinary
The warm morning was quiet
Suddenly I started drooling out of my mouth
Things were not mantling right

HANDS TIED

How does a Deaf poet sign
and end up with unintended umlauts
of which mispronunciations
are unheard of
especially if not recited by hands?

But how could a Deaf poet
end up with
a written commotion
as chaotic
as a metric foot
in his mouth?

As if sound is by rote
assonant by assimilation
of which pronunciations
are deftly arresting
by umlauts
by insinuendo.

WORDS

How would you extrapolate a thought?
How would you explain an idea?
How would you express feelings?
How would you exchange intellectively
enmeshed in such ravaged minds?

It's all a matter of words.

How would you cascade a thought?
How would you conjure an idea?
How would you convey feelings?
How would you comprise intellection
entangled in such rambunctious minds?

It's all a matter of words.

Words, huh?
Words, hmm.
W-O-R-D-S!
Words. Ah yes.

It's all a matter of words.

We live through so many things.
We see so many things.
We feel so many things.
We hear so many things

It's all a matter of words.

We percolate.
We think.
We emulate.
We speak.

We articulate.
We write.
We gesticulate.
We sign.
We participate.

It's all about words.

NO FAIRY TALES

No fairy tales—
no fairy tales at all.
None to remember.
None to retell.

Yet, I was amused
   when I read them
 as a kid.

And yes, I watched them
   on television, too.

My father was no king
nor was my mother a queen.
My brother was no prince
nor were my sisters, princesses.
Nor were there witches—
only lonely old ladies
wandering about the gutters.
Nor were there beggars—
only drunkards
         panning for another shot.

And,
there were no black cauldrons
and monstrous dragons around.

No. No fairy tales—
no fairy tales at all.
None to remember.
None to retell.

I'd tell you of New York City subways—
hardly tunnels of fear.

I'd tell you of great bridges over rivers—
too strong for scary thresholds.
I'd tell you of magnificent skyscrapers—
too gothic, too busy for romantic castles.
I'd tell you of fantastic rides and
adventuresome drives
in cars
and trucks
and buses
and trains
and planes—
comparatively too nice and comfortable
to a sleigh, a buggy
or a saddle.
If I had to decide which fairy tale
would be conceivably,
reasonably
unalterable
a life with my loving wife
with bushy brown hair
and two great kids—
wild and woolly—
eager to run.

No. No fairy tales—
no fairy tales at all.
None to remember.
None to retell.

Who would believe that
hereafter
we'd live ever so happily?

Gone Far, Still Goin'

THE A-TRAIN EXPRESS

Subway ride—
a shaky roll
underground—
beneath the bustling metropolis—
the grand Gotham
constantly pricking
at the sky.
Pressing even harder—
standing on a singular rock
in the bay.

No vehicle
or pedestrians
on the streets
quake us below.

The bedeviling ride—
flittering lights
in the dark tunnels—
like fire at peak
from every bright and dim
pale yellow
(or is it grimy white?)
then ultraviolet
and then red light
between 59th and 125th
and fenced-out by
listless beams—
whisked lights
flash-passing
non-stop
countlessly.

Relief.
Relief comes at a station stop.
Alighting and boarding—
rolling stiles
and running files.

JUST A DAY AWAY

I strolled by the lake
By the farm
Around the corner
From the house—
I had my camera
Ready to shoot
A wading merganser
Who distantly had no patience
For such a slow shutter.

I saw a lazy Siberian tiger
At the National Zoo
Who laid so stoic.
Locked up in an enclosure
Staring at the awning throng
Yawning at the boring beautiful day.
Her graciousness had long dwindled
Waiting for her next meal
Served without much ado.

A pink rose blossomed
At the Butchart Garden
Crowded with kibitzers
On a sunny day
After the misty whiff
To bathe her petals—
I gave her a brief reprieve
From the glaring sun—
She blinked her eye, pink.

I walked along Broadway
from ol' Herald Square
To find the landmark
I had not seen

Since I moved away—
NYC is not home anymore.
All the enticing forked words
That smoked out of Camels
Have long gone out of time.

Gone Far, Still Goin'

ON CASCO BAY

While strolling down the Riverwalk
a tanker slowly moaned by
speedboats fleeing by
the lobstermen have long been gone
long ago in the morning
but nary a ripple
      rapped the riverbanks

Hand in hand with my love
with no one else
walking down the Riverwalk
hand in hand

Merging Sun
far over and between the islands
on the calm rocky bay
awaiting to be churned about

Lobster trap markers
buoy-mark the color-pocked bay
standing piles remember
fierce Atlantic summer storms

Hand in hand
on a yellow ferry ride
passing storm-fallen trees
sleepy ferns drooping
from the ebbing tides
      everyone's waiting to jump in
        the cool bay waters

Hand in hand with my love
with no one else
riding the yellow ferry
      hand in hand

THE HIGHER I WENT

I've climbed many a mountain
I've climbed many a mountain
She took me up so high—
Well, every time I reached
for the sky
it never seemed to be there.

I've climbed many a mountain
I've climbed many a mountain
She took me down to the valleys
Well, every time I reached
for the trees
the flowers were still in bloom.

Gentle winds
Alpine sun
Scuttling marmots
Pondering clouds
Boulder jags
Snowcapped crags
Falling boulders roll
Mounting screes
Glaciating ice fields
Embalming streams
Well, that's the Athabasca way.

I've climbed many a mountain
I've climbed many a mountain
Well, the higher I went
her gcntlc winds
carried me away.

ON HENRY LAWSON'S
LONELINESS
BY THE DARLING

It was one of those nights
his mates gathered around
the raging comforting campfire
yarning and yapping
and having a few drinks.

The night was dark
too dark for Henry to see
mustached lips jawing
stubble and bearded faces jowly
roasting in the evening fire.

He called it a typical night
lit by a full moon
dancing candlelights weren't sprightly
unforgiving shadows
darkened faces like

masquerading masks
in the bleak blackened night.
He entered his tent
collapsed on his unrolled sack
rested his head on his hands
crossed his stretched legs
staring at the sheer ceiling
catching shadows of boughs
full of leaves
sweeping in the winds

teasingly brushing the rooftop—
staring at the dancing moonlight
urging for the brightest starlight
cascading cajoling thoughts
what will tomorrow be.

*Note: Henry Lawson, a poet who was Deaf,
was born in Sydney, Australia.*

ODE TO HENRY LAWSON:
A ROLLING SEA CHANTY

Henry Lawson was a brave man.
As courageous as he has ever been
The odds against him were insurmountable!
He stood his grounds as to lift his spirits.
His vainglorious stance against those odds
Wasn't as deterrent as they should have been.
He kept his promise and trodden the bush—
Swag, bottle, and pen.

Henry Lawson was an angry man.
As ostentatious as he has ever been
The odds against him were insurmountable!
He stood his grounds as to lift his spirits.
His exegetical scores against those odds
Weren't so deterrent as they should have been.
He kept his promise and wrote as he saw—
Swag, bottle, and pen.

Henry Lawson was a lonely man.
As misanthropic as he has ever been
The odds against him were insurmountable!
He stood his grounds as to lift his spirits.
His euphemisms against those odds
Weren't so deterrent as they should have been.
He kept his promise and fended his radical thoughts—
Swag, bottle, and pen.

Henry Lawson was a deaf man.
As humane as he has ever been
The odds against him were insurmountable!
He stood his grounds as to lift his spirits.
His fury against those odds
Weren't so deterrent as they should have been.
He kept his promise and tramped the wallaby—
Swag, bottle, and pen.

ABOUT THE TALE OF AN OLD BAY FISHERMAN

Have you ever gone
someplace near the Bay
and tried to sit by a grumpy,
whiskered,
whiskey-nosed,
lispy lipping leper
of a reddened,
sunbaked,
waveslapped,
windsogged,
thick-skinned fisherman
far from his windjamming days
amid the odorous
decaying deadfish, seafresh air
listening to the tales
of crab grabbing, oyster hoist-raking
days
gazing agape,
with mesmeric awe—
thunderstruck by his filthy
weather-worn
yellow-stemmed,
fierce face-carved
blackened white
meerschaum pipe
clenched between his tobacco-stained,
shellcracked,
rope-battened teeth—

Gone Far, Still Goin'

shucking bluefins and
occasional oysters
with rapid sleight
of water-thickened,
short-stumped,
fat-fingered,
bare hands?

LOW TIDE!
SLOW ROLLING SWELLS!
FOG ROLL!

Low tide!
Slow rolling swells!
Fog roll!
Schooner
ghosting a Maine bay.

A crew blows his conch horn
a reckoning warning:
steering full and by
tacking her course
dead ahead.

Low tide!
Slow rolling swells!
Fog roll!
Schooner
ghosting a Maine bay.

A crew blows his conch horn
a reckoning warning:
refurbished—
Modernized 19th century
full-mast schooner ahead.

Low tide!
Slow rolling swells!
Fog roll!
Schooner
ghosting a Maine bay.

Gone Far, Still Goin'

Lobster trap buoys
lay still on
the rolling bay waters
out of her past.

Low tide!
Slow rolling swells!
Fog roll!

Gulls, loons, cormorants
perch high on bare seaweeded
barnacle musseled
sea-horned rocks

Lost sunshine
Moon and Star
hidden in the mist of mystery

Low tide!
Slow rolling swells!
Fog roll!

Schooner
ghosting a Maine bay.

OCEAN DRIVE

The sea breezes
      were strong—
a hint of an approaching storm—
      a northbound hurricane.

High tides were rushing
          over the dunes
      ramping the jetties—
a raging tempest
          throwing tantrums.

An inundated tern
      on the bridge.

BENJAMIN'S INQUISITION AT SEVEN YEARS OF AGE

What makes the wind?
    What makes the wind?
        Daddy, what makes the wind?

For I all know—
    I don't really know,
and I can't tell him that!
    It wouldn't make a difference to him
anyway.

What makes the wind?
    Daddy, what makes the wind?
        Daddy, the book tells me about
                the sea,
           the land,
       the sky,
     the clouds,
but
        Daddy, what makes the wind?
        I don't get it.

The marvel.
    The magic.
    The mysterious.
        The magnificent.
           The wondrous.
             The wind.
    The wind?

The wind,
        Daddy, the wind,
        what makes the wind?

What makes the wind?
        Daddy,
        what makes the wind?

The sea.
        The land.
                The sky.
                        The clouds.
                They work together, y'know?
                        The warm fronts,
                                the cold fronts,
                                        y'know?

                When they come together,
                                they all work together,
                                        y'know?

The wind,
        Daddy, the wind,
        what makes the wind?

SNOWY THANKSGIVING AT DEEP CREEK LAKE

O Whirl!
    O Whirl!
        O Whirl! O Whirl!
           O Wind!
      The Wind!
      The Wind!
      The Wind!

High in the Appalachians
    Retreating to Tranquility
        despite the snowfalls
    and icy winds.

O Whirl!
    O Whirl!
        O Whirl! O Whirl!
           O Wind!
      The Wind!
      The Wind!
      The Wind!

Flurries after flurries
upstaged snow
    swept out of grace
        eddied to a
           quieter repose.

O Whirl!
    O Whirl!
        O Whirl! O Whirl!
           O Wind!

The Wind!
The Wind!
The Wind!

Skimming across the Lake—
        distorting the shadows
                of a cloud-bursting Sun—
                        Beatified Solace.

                                O Whirl!
        O Whirl!
                O Whirl! O Whirl!
                        O Wind!
                The Wind!
                The Wind!
                The Wind!

High in the Appalachians
        cherishing the commodious placidity
                despite the snowfalls
        and icy winds.

O Whirl!
        O Whirl!
                O Whirl! O Whirl!
                        O Wind!
                The Wind!
                The Wind!
                The Wind!

Gone Far, Still Goin'

DEATH AND THE DEVIL AT MY DOOR

Running with the storm
    reaping the sea.

Rolling waves riding kneading tides!
    kneading tides!

Kneading tides!
    Higher and higher.
        Harder and harder.

Rushing to the shores
    ripping the dunes
        rockbashing fiery splashes
rapping at my door.

        Rapping at my door—
running with the storm
    reaping the sea.

        Rising swells riding kneading tides!

Rolling waves riding
    kneading tides!
        Kneading tides!

Rapping at my door.
    Rapping at my door.

Death at my door
        running with the storm
    reaping the sea.

The Devil at sea
                    rapping at my door.
              Rapping at my door.
        Rapping at my door.

        Roaring Waves!
              Surging Waves!
                    Rushing Waves
                  running with the storm
                        reaping the sea.
                              Just as
                              sudden
                                    when
                                    it
                                    began
                        just as quick
                    just a quick swish
              of an unsteady moored mast—
                    like the magic wand
              a deathly calm
        the Sun leaps up.

        The clouds fade away

Licking laps—
        lapping
        lapping
        lapping open wounds ashore
              stroking dunes.

Still forcefully rockbashing
        fiery splashes

              Death and the Devil
        have gone to sleep.

ALL IN A GROUP

All in a group in loop
meditating words of meditation
no words cited in recitation
Hearing I's say I's

and staring eyes at eyes
Eight in a group in loop

All in a group in loop

All in a group in loop
Each conveys feelings from heart
with words never before comparted
like stone-grinding stones
out from heart to bones
Eight in a group in loop

All in a group in loop

All in a group in loop
Thinking thoughts in mind
with words unrefined
and sharing yours with mine
as hearts intertwine
Eight in a group in loop

All in a group in loop

All in a group in loop
no feelings in deliberation

but life in rehabilitation
each mind to heart
what never before I's rampart
Eight in a group in loop

All in a group in loop

MINDNOTES

Taking a brisk walk around the campus
  seems like a healthy thing to do,
      instead of sitting
              in the cluttered office
      pouting, and then,
pecking the computer endlessly.

      I forgot now.
              Minute details in
                      the moment of need—
  gone.
              It was so good.
  It was such a good thought
                      what was it?

      Professorial duties—
              I'm always thinking—
  improvising ways of making things
              happen in and out of the classroom.

      So much to say,
              so little time.
  so much to do, so little
                      space.

      Forget it. I'll take a walk.

              My head bowed, with every step taken
      listlessly staring at every walkway line,
every gum patch, every tree well, and
once in a while, every brick—until
there's cadence or two
      or until
      there's a burst of scholarly euphoria.

COMPETITION

Momma Robin comes
       bobbin' on the wood deck;
Grey Squirrel grooms himself
           on the corner
           on the railin',
   meanwhile.

     Her breast lacked a red sheen—
          she's pregnant.
     Ah, yeah. Sprin' in spruce
        or just about.
     The cold is still about.

     She
pecks 'n bobs 'n
    pecks 'n bobs 'n
        pecks 'n bobbin'
  for seeds 'n nuts spurned—
  scattered on the wood deck.

     Grey Squirrel runs down the railin',
      hops about—
  rustlin' about the hulls 'n shells—
    nibblin' whatever he finds
        on the wood deck.

Momma Robin bobs about
keepin' her distance—
        she pecks 'n bobs 'n
    pecks 'n bobs 'n
   peck 'n bobbin'
   about
  'n flies away.

THEY FLOCK

At every instinctive
chance they flock
when others could meet.

They seek and seek
when all alone
in need to flock.

When they clutch
feathers stifle
pluck and preen
in the rut to roost.

A shift in time
a scent of air—
an urge to meet.

Like birds—
        they swish wings—
the urge to flock.

Like sea turtles—
        they swish flippers—
the urge to roost.

At any waft
or whiff—they
flock where
others would roost.

At the rookery
where they roost
when they flock
hands fly.

FOSSIL HUNTING AT CALVERT CLIFFS

Chesapeake Bay
by the eastern shore—
scavengers and hunters
wade through stories, shells,
and bones awash,
and uprooted naked trees—
looking for sea fossils
but yielding to sea weather,
becoming conspicuous
by the limestone cliffs—
        back in the wet dark.

1987: YEAR OF THE CICADA

We had some strange visitors
whom we've never met before.
They came by the millions—
hardly a place did they miss;
even their empty shells clung
to practically anything.
They flew about the yard,
squatted on the trees,
thumped against the windshields,
were squashed under the tires,
and Ben had the joy of stepping
on them, too. And oh yes, even
Rebecca—cute little one—
played the cook.

Curtis Robbins

LITTLE BIRD

Little bird, little bird
you must fly
you must fly
with the wind,
with your wings wide

Little bird, little bird
you must fly
you must fly
to the treetop
to the treetop
not as far as Pegasus
but with the wind,
with your wings wide

Little bird, little bird
you must fly
you must fly
in the air
in the air
with the wind,
with your wings wide

Gone Far, Still Goin'

SPEECHLESS MIND

How odd it is to write
    nothing or about nothing—
        the slump has long gone
            by the adrenergic way
                of exacerbating
                dreams.

           Writer's cramps
        from persistently pecking
      away at keyboard
    wreaked spasms
of the hands.

      Painkillers only sedate
    words from scouring the screen.

           There's much processed
                memory rammed
           There's much decerebrate
                verses pixelated
           There's much imprinted
                imageries dried out

    The fork ran away with the spoon.

AFRAID

I am afraid of the sky—
an endless fall—
I'd be going down through
a cold, white abyss—
falling to the ever greening—
what will happen to me
when things get bigger?

I am afraid of the ladder—
the higher I step
the unsettlingly shakier it is
for a short fall—
falling to
a solid, cold floor—
too slow—
too soon
to figure out
how it would happen.

I am afraid of the roof of my house—
the slanted grade—
haphazard winds
make it difficult
to know whether to stand
against
or lean on the grade—
unpredictability
at graded heights.

I am afraid of the canoe—
it's designed without ballasts.
I cannot stand up, or
shift around so much—
grounded to a rocking confine—

nowhere near a certain hold—
even the dark, cold depths
that holds it up.

I am afraid of domineering women—
I've seen too many in my life
They are so disruptive—
having little or no compassion—
even for themselves.
What is worse than women
who shun men—even when men
encourage them to ascend?

I am afraid of overpowering men
who continue climbing to higher echelons—
they only know their hollow glories.
Forgetting those who helped them rise,
forgetting who their friends were—
remembering only their adversaries.

Because I won't climb,
I am afraid to be judged
(some people can't be trusted).

LONELY CAMARADERIE

Among cocktails and hors d'oeuvres
the cliquey clamoring
laughing ohs and ahs

Between chicanery and chatters
smacks and puckers
pattering about
handshakes and hugs
back patting and cheeky kisses

Spillages and near misses

Among clustering glamour
perfume and cologne
pompous pretensions
the cliquey clamoring

Pillages and oversights

Between cocktails and hors d'oeuvres
I hardly knew what they were
yet I managed to bite and sip
sidestepping a word edgewise.

ON HARPO MARX

For as long as I can remember
        since I was a kid watching
                the B&W Marx Brothers
                        movies on television.

It was hard to laugh
      at adult jokes
           no captions to depend on.

    It was even harder to laugh
          at adult jokes
               when nuances of
                    spoken words played.

            To laugh or not,
           I was smitten
        by that bright white-wigged
     guy who never said a word
   yet made so much noise
and I was able to tell
what a nuisance he was.

It was hard to laugh
at his intended jokes
because the bewildering
puns always
left me stunned.

        But, damn,
        it took so long
        to guffaw—
        pondering
        whether to do it or not—
        the delay was well meant.

Harpo's actions
    designated the contrary
        contradicting other contraries
            his two brothers meant
                for their own design.

                To explain them
           through his bells and whistles
        guessing the scheme of his actions
     in unspeakable words
    punctuated by subtle
visual noises
he cascades—
    only to perpetuate
        his contradictory contrarious intents
           that even spoken words
              were never really
                meant to be.

It was hard to laugh
at his intended jokes
because the bewildering
puns always
left me stunned.

    But, damn,
    it took so long
    to guffaw—
    pondering
    whether to do it or not—
    the delay was well meant.

Harpo—
        some of us should know
                was muted by
                        spoken contraries
                                that contradicted
                                        the initial intent.
Yet his hands
        spoke another language
                that even I could never
                        understand—
                                they danced
                                        on the strings
                                                of his harp

                or between his lips
                        between two fingers
                                a shriveling whistle—
                                        a visual
                                                I couldn't
                                        comprehend.

        But, damn,
                it took so long
                to guffaw—
                pondering
                whether to do it or not—
                the delay was well meant.

MAN AT
THE INTERSECTION OF
NEW YORK AVENUE AND
BLADENSBURG ROAD

Gimme a hug
Gimme a buck
I've run outta luck
'n no place t'tuck in.

The shoeless,
> jacketless A-A man,
> on a balmy mid-autumn morning,
> with his pants rolled up,
> paced the intersection of New York Avenue
> and Bladensburg Road
> on the middle southbound median—
waving good-naturedly
> with a definitive nudge—
> holding a rubbed-in
> boldfaced

HUNGRY HELP
PLEASE

torn-off corrugated box side sign.

Gimme a hug
Gimme a buck
I've run outta luck
'n no place t'tuck in.

Gone Far, Still Goin'

For pity's sake—
                  the shoeless,
          jacketless A-A man
          with his pants rolled up—
     he's telling
          the unflappable traffic
       at the traffic light:

             Gimme a hug
             Gimme a buck
            I've run outta luck
           'n no place t'tuck in.

ELECTION

Representation
    by popular votes
        split by partisan splats
            writhing through
                warped minds
                    blind-spotted
                        stout-hearted
                        by political
                        dogma.

Propaganda
    Indoctrination
        brainwashed by
            the implantation
                of seedy powers
                    to incite
                wrongful rights
                    electing
                who or what
        never
      deemed
    right.

GUTTERSNIPE

Professor Higgins found Eliza
    at her Cockney best
        selling flowers
            for her reaps
                at the Covent Garden.

Professor Higgins found a specimen
    in her in her rawest moment
        utterly unprepared
            to be a beguiled
                Cinderella

        without that
        bibbidi-bobbidi-boo
            she's what he reaps
                to make her think
            it's a *bibbidi-bobbidi-boo*!

With all that *boolera*
    his professorial cockiness
        never brought about the magic.

        When midnight struck at the Ascot races
            Eliza was at her Cockney best
        When midnight struck at the Embassy Ball
            Eliza was at her Cockney best.

Bibbidi-bobbidi-boo!

All that *boolera*
    made her unhappy ever after!

I was born in the gutters of NYC and the woods
of Long Island—
    living in the confines of comfort
            warm homes
            plentiful food
            nightly baths
            clean clothes
            public schools

Professor Higgins found a specimen
        in my rawest moments
                in those lifelong never-ending
                speech therapy sessions
                        with all my inborn
                        mouthful of marbles.

Poor Professor Higgins
        his magic had no *boolera*
                but my *boolera* did prevail.

When midnight struck at the Delta Epsilon Dance
                I was the dreamboat at my signing best!
    When midnight struck at the bridge table
                I was acing kings at my signing best!

Bibbidi-bobbidi-boo!

MR. WASHINGTON AND
I GO A LONG WAY BACK

I was born in Washington Heights
    several blocks away from the
    George Washington Bridge.
        Dad was raised a few blocks down by the Wall.
           He graduated from George Washington
           High School.

I was born in the same month as George
    and for a while, raised in the Heights during WW II
        when Dad was in the service
           and Mom had to work—
                at least we always
                    had portraits of George
                      in our pockets.

I fantasized, listening to the story of the chopped cherry tree
    and the silver dollar that never quite
        made it across the Rappahannock
        and dreamt of riding his great white horse
           but shuddered at the thought
                of crossing the wintry Delaware.

I graduated from Gallaudet College in Washington DC
    visited the Washington Monument
        and the Smithsonian Museum
           where the lionized statue of
              the naked George
              who was thought of as
                  the King of the USA
                  is hidden out of
                    embarrassment.

And I often went to the National Art Gallery
                    where the portrait of the young, tall
                         General George Washington
                              hung.

I frequented Georgetown
        where Mr. Washington's mom dwelled.
            I interned at Mount Vernon
                saw his wooden teeth
                     guarded his deathbed
                          and stood by the burial
                          mound
                               contemplating
                               everything—
                     idolizing him.

And even pitched a tent
        for an overnight camp
            out by his birthplace
                in Westmoreland.

Of course, I had to go to the outhouse—
            there was a carved engraving:
                George sat here!

I now teach at George Washington University
        I pass his bust every day
            with a pocketful of his portraits
                and occasionally crossed the bridge
                     there was never a dull moment
                          knowing—
                          remembering him.

Gone Far, Still Goin'

RERUNS ON TELEVISION

Filmic evidence of past wars—
    emblazoned on television immemorially
        reminding,
            rescinding,
                or provoking
          one for tomorrow?

Nations rise
    and Nations fall
        in remunerative ways
           between clashes
                  of rises and
                      falls
                 of others.

Nations heighten the ante,
        and fall at will of whims—
           Defeat is only an aftertaste
           Victory embalms
           and vice versa.

Contention
        is the joy of
          antagonizing
      the less contented
        (often agitating the equally contented)
      testing untested remunerations
        misfortunes and fortunes
          en masse.

To those who survived
       misdeeds and deeds of war—
          reliving by watching
                    what theories
                    belie history
              to underscore
              memories
              on TV.

AIN'T NOBODY THERE FOR ME?

No, there ain't nobody around.

I could be standing next to a guy
who's hearing a PA announcement.
I could tell when someone is making
an announcement but not what he's saying.
If I ask this guy what was said
he'd say—as always—
nothing important
or
not sure
or
I dunno.

No, there ain't nobody around.

I could be standing next to a lady
who's hearing a commotion.
I could tell when something is happening
and everyone is running and screaming.
If I ask this lady what is going on
she'd say—as always—
Something happened
or
Oh something or other
or
I don't know.

No, there ain't nobody around.

Curtis Robbins

I'm all alone in the middle
of a thrashing, bashing crowd
on the run like a parade in disarray.
There's no knowing
where to go
or
what to find
or
who to ask.

Ain't No Sounds There For Me?

No, there ain't nobody around.

I'm all alone in the band.
There ain't nothing to toot or woof a horn
and
there ain't nothing to pluck or strum a guitar
and
there ain't nothing to bow or rappel a bass
and
there ain't nothing to dance or clap about
and
No way could I sing.

No, there ain't nobody around.

Sounds around abound
so noisily so. I cannot know
what they are
or
where they come from

or
wonder why people are
always running about
and can't tell me
what they're all about

No, there ain't nobody around.

THIS DEAF-MUTE BOY
WHO COULD'VE

There was once
    a five-and-a-half-year-old precocious Deaf kid
        who was taken to tryout
            for a little league baseball team.

He was among the 50-plus kids
    whose daddies thought their sons were the best.

The Deaf kid tried out for catcher
    and turned out to be the best—
        even his daddy thought so, too.

The coaches were quite impressed
    by the Deaf kid's abilities
        to bat, catch, and throw.

The coaches gathered
    to declare the choicest of the bunch.

Names of each kid were called
    but the Deaf kid
        who was so good
            was, for sure, the catcher
                for the new team
                    stood waiting—
knowing he was really so good.

A few times the Deaf kid's name
    was called
        but each time there was no response.

Gone Far, Still Goin'

A coach finally came over
    asked the Deaf kid
        where's your daddy
            the Deaf kid waved for Daddy to come.

The smiling coach said a thing or two
    but there was no response—
        Daddy was deaf, too!

Daddy pulled his pad and pencil
    from his shirt pocket
        and wrote asking the startled coach
            please write what he said—

This deaf-mute boy cannot play baseball.

HE'S DEAF
FOR CHRISSAKES!

The light bulb glows
    when the sky darkens

    The jack-o'-lantern laughs
        when the candle dims

        The gourd keeps shape
            when gracefully empty

            The balloon dances airily
                when tethered to ascend

                The cicada shells cling
                    when the seventeenth
                    year embarks

        The mind beacons
            when latent listen
            and rambunctious eyes seek

    The Deaf man stridulates
        when ignorance peaks

The Deaf man cries out
    when impertinence meets

The Deaf man sees
    when malice impugns

            He's deaf for Chrissakes!

DEAF PEDDLERS

...They sell the hollow
of their hands.
The Beggars, *Rainier Maria Rilke*

All day long (sometimes at night, too)
    on the streets
        or under
            the subways
    or at the getaways
        airports
                bus depots
                      train stations
    or at the eateries—
        they weren't even hungry

    they just go around
        handing out manual alphabet cards

        I AM DEAF
        PLEASE HELP

    then return to collect them again
        expecting some change with it.

After a good day's round
    they count
        their blessings.

When they get back to the Deaf club
    they rant and rant and rant
        sick and tired of hearing people
            feeling sorry for Deaf people.

ON TEACHING POETIC STRESS TO DEAF READERS

What hand paints the void,
    that metrically ascent

                        with an accent
               on poetic stress?
Nary is a voice ever heard
        (nor phantomized by some fantasized notion)
    nor an articulated word
        in its questionable pronunciation
           could one know
             the precepts of
        poetic stress.

How, by sight if not by sound
    may one grasp
        conjecturing syllables
           heightened by a certain
       earmarked meter
         depicting poetic stress?

And how may I,
        a deaf poet nonetheless
           teach accented sounds
             to deaf readers
         attempting to appreciate poetry?

WHEN I COMPOSE

Sometimes after gazing at
        the infinity of light
sometimes after reading other poems
        stories or anecdotes
sometimes after recalling an incident
        or a personal situation
sometimes after looking at myself
    a strange commotion stirs
        somewhere down deep—
            I am lost.

When I compose a poem,
        there's nothing to think about
with a pen and paper
        or on the computer—
    words flow out as if
            tapped from a faucet.

And even then,
        words are sometimes misused.
I'd seek a dictionary or a thesaurus
        to imbibe the meaning accordingly.
Yet,
    in the deepest of my deepest
the dark fathoms of glory—
        a canvas
of words
        a picture from a palette
        and a paintbrush to compose.

And so, when I compose,
   I stare at the void
of my soul—
      the stark, cold
fathoms of glory—
      words
     in the eyes
     of my mind.

I see,
    then, I saw.

Intangibility—
    words only paint my mind
    letting my hands guide the flow.

DEAF POET OR WHAT?

They keep asking the same question:
"Are you a Deaf Poet
or
A poet who is Deaf?"
I shudder at the question.
I can't even think of a better way
To express the rhetoric.
I'm lost.
Did I mention anything otherwise?
Did I falter at my wordsmithing?
Did I recant something so obvious?
Did I wreak poetic havoc?
Who am I?
or rather
What am I?
"Did you sign?"
or
"Do you sing?"
or
"Do you truly hear such peripatetic words?"
The matter doesn't warrant an answer—
I am what you read.

A DEAF BILINGUAL POET'S DILEMMA

Dilemma:
>I've written so many poems
>and have been wanting so badly
to recite them before an audience

>>The trouble is
>if I verbalize them
>there's always this hearing audience
>>who may not understand me—
>but I know, my deaf friends,
>>they'd be piqued
>if I don't sign to them as well.
>>(The secret is, I can't
>>>sign with such *pas de deux*.)

Dilemma:
>I can't do both simultaneously,
>>or I'll recant poetic decorum.
>So what shall I do with my audience?

Dilemma:
>When I compose
>>I don't think
>in terms of how
>>my hands should flow
>>>or how my speech should carry
>>>just so
>>to appeal to the audience.

Dilemma:
     My mind is my audience
     and then again, it is my mouthpiece.
         But then again,
        I've never thought
    with reconnoitering hands.
So, what shall I do with my audience?

Dilemma:
     Will all my readers be there?

POETS WINING AND DINING

There's a table
full of poets
    feasting—
        binging
            on recitations
                in meters
                feet
                rhythm
            and rhyme.

Ten yapping men
    jabbing cadences
        at the candle cups.

        Ten lipless faces
           laughing
                in silhouettes
                    in the dimmed dark.

Ten rowdy clowns
    cascading chairs
        pounding fists
            limping the tables.

Ten jiving silhouettes
    pricking—
        macerating the already
           dulled spotlights.

There's a platter
of tape cassettes
and a whining parade
of rattling
emptied bottles

marching
at the beat
of the guffawing
tables
and ten plates
full of silence
for the blank night.

As a Deaf poet
it makes no sense
for me to join
the fray.

Curtis Robbins

BENJAMIN'S BRIS

My first-born son
eight days old

The mohel chants:
given a life,
circumcise him
to welcome
the newborn Jew.

The little one—
he wails from the pain
at the chant for the wine:

borei pere hagafen

Hallelujah.

Hallelujah!

REBECCA'S DISLIKE OF SLEEPING ON HER BED

Rebecca,
at her age of 4,
doesn't know
when to stop
smiling.

Now.
    Later.
        Ah, likely never.
            Come night.

"Daddy, it's dark outside,"
    she said matter of factly—
        pointing out the window.

"Yes, my sweet," I responded,
        pretending
        I didn't know.

"But, Daddy, I don't wanna go t'sleep now."

"Well, tomorrow's another day.
    Now, go t'bed."

        "Daddy!"
She stomps her right foot
with her arms akimbo,
looking coldly at me.

She runs off, angrily,
grabbing one of her dolls

from the kitchen floor,
    and a dish towel
    from the refrigerator door,
and into the living room.
    Turns one lamp off
    and leaves the other on.

        Sitting on the couch,
          she, carefully,
          wraps her doll—
              lullabying
          herself to sleep.

        I guess it's better
        than aggravating myself
              tucking her in—
          trying to sing to her.

REBECCA'S ART

Every day, without much ado,
    she grabs whatever
                  is available to her—
        without lifting from the paper
          whatever is in her hand—
             drawing lines.

Fills the intersecting
              (and often bisecting)
                perpendiculars
                  and
            haphazard geometric
                asymmetries
           with hues of bright
               rainbow colors.

When she's done—
        it's not when her artwork
              is finished,
    she'd cut, staple, roll, and fold,
        and holepunch 'em, sometimes—
           it's where she puts 'em.

Now, go about the house
        and look among the clutter.

Go in the kitchen,
    look by the microwave
        on the serving counter.

Then, go to the other counter
    by the window near the stove,

look in the box
by the rice cooker
next to the breadmaker.

Yes, they're practically all over the place.

Go in the living room,
look around long couch,
behind it,
under it;
look between the cushions,
behind it,
beneath them.

Indeed, they're all over the place.

Y'know, the art—
Rebecca's art is not
what or how she draws or
what or how she consolidates
but where she puts them—
a child's work of art.

POPCORN
FOR BREAKFAST

Rebecca wanted popcorn for breakfast!

Of course, I said, "No."

                  She stomped
        her right foot
Desperately crying
    "I
      want
         pop-
            c o r n,"
    continually stomping her feet,
clinching and pulling—
    jerking at my left
        dungarees pocket.

Again, I said, "No."

All the while,
    I wondered
        whatever happened to
           "Snap, Crackle, and Pop?"
        Such is a decent
    bowl of cereal
        for breakfast.
           Or was it?

TO MY BROTHER

Grief has overtaken us
    in strange ways—
        Grief lingers
            then escapes.

Your passing fills idle moments
    with sweet memories
        of your mischievous laughter—
            ageless cackles for your
        devious impish teasing.

Sibling rivalry was such a minor spurt of youth
    the four of us celebrated life
        as we've always known it—
            we still laughed at each other's
                evolving foibles.

But your untimely departure
    brought anger
        confusion
            frustration—
reasons have long been dissipated
when we couldn't find you—
                you were, indeed,
        unknown
      unnamed
and numbered.

Where were we when
you truly needed us?

Your cries were long silenced
when we couldn't find you.

Friends
colleagues
and relatives
       how we grieved!

Your goodness
       your heart
              and yes, even
                     your resounding cackles
                            are still heard

now that we found you.

SUSAN LYNN

It never was a dream

                                    nor a reality.
            We've been together for so long—
       We rejoiced every moment—

                          we reveled in love.

Pangs of miscalculated judgments

                     purveyed mutual respect.
           Whether the bills,
       or matters of the children,
       or situational disagreements—
           petty arguments—
           such tensions simmer
               in agreement,
                     and again,
           we reveled in love.
And deviant temptations
           were always mollified
           by my thoughts of you.

          There once was a woman who
               crossed my path
                and truly
                crossed me—
        trying to rape
        the bliss that keeps us,
             you and me,
         close together.

We give and take for each other—
          you and me.
We rejoiced in every moment—

          we reveled in love.   Happiness
doesn't best describe this.

A DEAF SCOTTISH LADY COMES TO AMERICA

A long way from Glasgow to Baltimore—
                a long way from the sophistication
                        of a natural habitat:
                                her familiarities,
                                her customs,
                                her language—

Her ways are of ingrained simplicity—
                        her old country style;
                the America she perceived
                                behooves her,
                        she's frustrated
                                by the complexities
                                        compounded

                        utterly unScottish

To migrate was once a powerful dream
                to escape a free country,
                        to break from a clan,
                                to deride a culture,
                                        to pull roots
                        and run with lost pride,
                                        knowing so few,
                and estranged from her
        already dispersed family.

Nothing sweet remembered.
    Nothing bittersweet rebuked—
        soured by betrayal.
    Embittered by betrayal.
  Bitter, still, by betrayal.

        She goes home.

TECHNOLOGY
OF SILENCE

The technology of silence…
Do not confuse it
with any kind of absence
    Cartographies of Silence, *Adrienne Rich*

I noticed
my children sat quietly together
        on the living room sofa
    gazing at the deepest end of the floor.
            The TV was off.

    My friend's dog, Shayna,
            lay by the stereo set
        nothing fazed her—
            the turntable wasn't turning.

Afterwhile,
Rebecca fell asleep
    even though the bright afternoon sun
            beamed from the picture window
                of the opposite wall.

Ben, at the armrest,
        paid no mind—
            far too preoccupied.

I walked by the tilt-top round table
        by the sofa,

where
                    a deep-bass,
                    dual-speakered
            portable AM/FM radio
and
            audiocassette player
                    played
                    a tape.

I touched it to make sure.

It was so loud.

Gone Far, Still Goin'

I REMEMBER

I remember Grandma, bless her
         she called me *mein yiddishe cuppe*
         though I'd never ask
I figured I was her favorite lil' boy.

I remember Mom—
         she called me Greenhorn
            I never had to ask
         I hated the broken
            green peas on my plate.

I remember Grampa, bless him—
         he called me a *meshugenuh*
             because I was
         a pain in his neck.

I remember asking Dad,
         What's a *meshugenuh*?
            (though I didn't say it correctly then)
    As usual he'd respond with a
         Cur-tis, stop hockin' me t'Chiny
            with such stupid questions—
               flailing his hands in anger
    (I guessed he didn't know it either).

I remember breaking a leg
    and coming home in a cast—
         Gramma stood there
         shaking her head with
            a hand on her cheek,
               bellowing

Curtis Robbins

Ay, ay, ay, ay, ay,
Why are you such a meshugenuh?!
Ay, ay, ay, ay, ay,
Meshugenuh!

I finally understood and laughed with a shrug.

THE STUDY

A very small room
in the basement—
big enough a place for
solace,
     refuge
          solitude—
always a place
to devour the books
and
to tinker with the computer.

FENCE ME NO MORE

Before I built a wall I'd ask to know
What I was walling in or walling out.
And to whom I was like to give offence.
Something there is that doesn't love a wall,
That wants it down.

Mending Wall, *R. Frost*

An old three-foot chain fence
was up long before we moved in.
To play in yard you must stay within, I'd explain—
though I dislike fences,
they limit the children's range

When they learned of my two children,
the disgruntled old couple came out,
attached a makeshift fence
from a stack of splintered—
stages to the existing fence
nearly three feet higher
with rust nails protruding.

One day, Benjamin inadvertently threw
a ball, intended for Rebecca,
over the fence—I was watching.
Out came the frail old lady,
angrily standing by the fence,
with a cold stare at the children—
thrust her middle fucking finger!

DAYDREAMS

In my early school days
    I learned to be a daydreamer—
        often participating in class
        was such a waste of time!

Alice and Jerry readers
    were rather easy to read
        but Teacher kept telling me
        to follow through—
            I hadn't the slightest notion
            where in the book to look!
                I just kept reading it
                over and over to myself
                and then I glimpsed at
                the penmanship cards
                above the blackboard.

    Teacher called upon me
    to read the next line!

            Huh? What?
            Where? Huh?

                I'm still on page 3
                the class on page 10

    Curtis! You're not paying attention!
        How was I supposed
        to know if I couldn't hear
        anyone reading aloud?

In junior high
    I became a pretty good daydreamer.
    I began seeing abstract imageries
    looking at the scheme of things
    around the classroom
        and out the window—
            still participating in class
            was such a waste of time!

The class was reading
"The Devil and Daniel Webster"

        but Teacher kept telling me
        to follow through—
            I hadn't the slightest notion
            where in the book to look!
                I read the story
                in its entirety and
                watched the clouds
                meander across
                the morning sky.

Teacher called upon me
to read the next paragraph
about the jury selections
in the courtroom!

        Huh? What?
        Where? Huh?

            I'm still on page 213
            the class on page 216.

Curtis! You're not paying attention!

What was I supposed to do?
Teacher knew I couldn't hear.

Even Principal originally presumed
            I was slow—
            not that I couldn't learn
                        they didn't want to be
                        bothered with my handicaps.

Yet, in high school
I was already an excellent daydreamer—
any thought that came to mind
was worth implosive sensualities
in my wildest dreams—
            well, participating in class
            was such a waste of time!

                  The class delved into "Julius Caesar."
                  Teacher, in his song-and-dance routine,
                  recited Marc Anthony's speech in attempts
                  to introduce Shakespeare.

The class followed
I was totally lost
but Teacher kept telling me
to follow through—
            I didn't have the slightest notion
            where in the book to look!
                        I read the play
                        one act at a time and
                        in between watching
                        how Teacher
                        zigzagged around the room.

Teacher called upon me
    to read what Brutus did
    before his suicide.

Huh? What?
                Where? Huh?

                            I'm still on page 112
                            the class on page 128

Curtis! You're not paying attention!

Et tu Brute?

DREAM

Early one morning
I woke up
I couldn't sleep
I had a strange dream.
                    It wasn't like
             any other one
       that I've had.

It struck me
       like dark lightning—
             a jolt to awaken me.

I climbed out of bed
and peeked out the window
between the blinds
watching the descending
       crescent moon
              looking for the rising sun
                 looking for Morning

Where am I?
I am all alone.
Where am I?
Everyone is home.

It was a cold night
the dark distant lightning
It was the darkest night
I couldn't see the rising sun.
I couldn't see Morning.

I'm all alone.
My children are asleep.
My dear wife is asleep—
everybody is home.

My pillow is empty
The ruffled corner of my bedside
Red beams from the alarm clock
keeps rolling the moments.
What's keeping me up?

Trees in a parade
of unmitigated rustles
tantalizing beacons
breaking streetlights
no car or pedestrian could go by
looking for the rising sun
looking for Morning.

Where am I?
I am all alone.
Where am I?
Everybody is home.

It was a cold night
the dark distant night lightning struck
It was the darkest night

I see the rising sun.
I couldn't see Morning.

I stood by the riverbank
watching the oceanward flow
wash away the glistening ripples

of the descending crescent moon
looking for the rising sun
looking for Morning.

Where am I?
I am all alone.
Where am I?
Everybody is home.

It was a cold night
the dark distant night lightning struck
It was the darkest night
I see the rising sun.
I couldn't see Morning.

I stood on a berm
looking for my Deaf friends
they were all around
in this sycophantic moment
muttering with clenched hands
looking for the rising sun
looking for Morning.

Where am I?
I am all alone.
Where am I?
Everybody is home.

It was the strangest cold night
the darkened moon shone.
It was the darkest night
I see the rising sun.
I couldn't see Morning.

LEARNING UP FRONT

For as long as I remember
I've always
I sat up front of the class
so I could watch Teacher
otherwise, I'd be sitting
in the back somewhere
reading lips
between bobbing, swaying, nodding heads:
some were tall
some were fat
some had perms wide or high
some had bushy ducktails or ponytails
some even had crewcuts
that the rest of the lesson didn't matter

As long as I sat up front
so I could watch Teacher.

Some teachers
talked chalkpoking the blackboard
Some teachers
talked flipping fanning pages
Some teachers
talked zigzagging rows of aisles
that bobbing, swaying, nodding
heads didn't matter

As long as I sat up front
so I could watch Teacher
When my classmates spoke
I never knew who
as long as I sat up front
so I could watch Teacher.

Gone Far, Still Goin'

Whether meticulously copious notes were
written on the blackboard or
on blue on white
nauseating ammoniated ditto or
on black on white
ink-botted, letter-smudged
mimeograph or
read from the book

As long as I sat up front
so I could watch Teacher.

ON MY SIXTIETH BIRTHDAY

Today
I looked at my
cracked mirror
at the horror of the thought

not the fact that I'm
losing that spry of youthfulness—
from the lost elasticity of my already wrinkling skin
and the thinning of my
already receded hairline
and the bulging of the already
lengthening beltline

nor the fact that my
masculinity has waned
to the diminutive
and the fact that my
virility is measured
by how much
I hold up
nor the fact
that the slow
aging process
has sped up

but the fact that I—
every morning—
still see that far
wondering—
what next?

DEAF CULTURE

Growing up different.
    Developing myself differently.
        Maturing to be different
            but not to be differentiated!

                How could we be so different?
ASL is beautiful.
    ASL is different
        ASL is differentiated
            by the lack of common modality
                that makes us so different
                    from the mainstream

        So, how could we be so different?

        Being Deaf makes us different.
            To be different, we must be Deaf.
            If not, then I'm
                unjustifiably deaf.

            How could we be so different?

No, it's not because hearing people are different
    and that they think differently from us
        but that they differentiate
        us from them
            whatever the case
                to them
            we are not the same
        we are Deaf.

It's the only difference
they see between us
and them.
So, how could we be so different?

Just because I can
commingle and immerse
and emulate the mainstream
does not make me
any different.

To be different
is to set
the differentiation—
which I have not!

How could we be so different?

Why should there be
differences between us?
What's a damned good reason
differentiating each other?
We've been fighting those
hearing people
to respect what
makes us
different.

So, how could we be so different?

Gone Far, Still Goin'

WHAT DOES THAT
MAKE ME?

Me? Deaf me?
Oh fuck, Y-E-S!

I don't live on a dividing line
or hang on a balance.
I never went to a school for the deaf
nor am I from a Deaf family.
I merely mainstreamed
through schools
with all the help I could get
to speak
to lipread
and to try to hear
which I never succeeded
even with those hearing aids
stashed in my proverbial brasserie
which were called "pockets" then
or with the ones hanging behind-the-ear.

Yet, I schooled and taught at Gallaudet.

But damn you
What's with you?
You should know
I'm D-E-A-F
with a capital D!

You ain't got no reason to say otherwise.
I know my ASL—I teach it.
Yeah, I can talk.

They can understand me fine!

I got me a Deaf wife—
who like me, can ASL (she teaches it, too)
and she talks, too.
We got two great CODAs
who can sign well enough just
to get their point across edgewise.

We got flashing systems
all over the house.
We got Deaf friends
and a handful of those who aren't.
So what?

So, damn you
What's with you?
You should know
I'm D-E-A-F
with a capital D!

Y-E-S!

HOW LOUD AM I REALLY?

A lot of times
    when the family
        goes out to eat
            I tend to
                say something
                    about darkened tables
                        in any restaurant.

No one would ever
let me tell them
it's too dark in there
anyway.
                    otherwise
            If I had to say anything else
        If the matter of importance
    doesn't take heed
they'd still hold me back.

                Shh. Shh.
            Hush. Hush.
                Shush. Shush.
                    Don't talk so loud.
                    Shh. Shh.

How loud is hush?
        How hush is shush?
How shush is shh?

Curtis Robbins

I never had a problem
with my hearing friends
and colleagues at the table
we always get by well
with laughter,
good conversation,
and hearty meals.

But here, with the family
I hardly ever have a chance to say
what I've been wanting to say.

when no one was willing
to listen anyway.

Shh. Shh.
Hush. Hush.
Shush. Shush.
Don't talk so loud.
Shh. Shh.

How loud is hush?

GAWKING BACK

It was a particularly uncomfortable
    moment in an elegant restaurant
    She was surely uneasy at what she saw:
        A Deaf guy signing to his Deaf wife.
        I had to reciprocate
            as if I've never really
            seen anyone behave
    like that before.

This pompous elderly lady
    she was something else,
        but you know what?

    I never wondered what
    thoughts she had about me.

A BRISK WALK IN
THE MIDNIGHT SNOW

Too restless to sleep
  Too wounded to lie down.
    Cataclysmic energy surging—
      nothing to jot down.

There's a snowstorm out there—
    I need to walk.
Yes. I'll go.

Blustery winds pushing and pulling
  hardly an easy step.

    Slush—
  tiny rocky
    mountains
   of ice,
      along the
      rolling hilly streets
   of my neighborhood

Tire tracks—
    snow track of
    icy impressions.

  My footsteps are covered
    with powdery snow.

Haunting footprints of snowbirds—
  blustery winds
    pushing and pulling—
      tracked in flight.

Bits of icy snow
                              from another storm—
                    fell from rooftops
              blown from trees,
          swept from snow dunes
rolling ahead of me.

HUH?

Some guy was standing
beside me
    talking
while he was flailing his hands—
of course, I didn't know
what he was saying.

He just kept on
yapping
yapping
yapping
while I was reading a mag.

Then we were
laughing together—
of course,

but I was laughing
at something I read
that was so funny.

My cochlear processor
by my left ear
was so obvious
he stood by
    that side of me.

That guy
he just kept on
yapping
yapping
yapping
and then he laughed again.

Gone Far, Still Goin'

Suddenly
Silence.

He elbowed me
I looked up
and then he asked
whatsa matter
didn't ya hear me?

WRONG CHOICES
IN LIFE

…having made the wrong choices in life,
it is an unacceptable insinuation to
someone who considers himself DEAF.
Deaf in America: Voices from a Culture, *Padden and Humphries*

Born hearing
    then became deaf
        by a doctor's error
            an overdose of
                an unknown drug
            what did he really know then?

I was barely a precocious kid then
    not even a year old as of yet
        who knew what it was like then?

I sucked my thumb
    it was a thing to do.
        Nobody bothered
            to ask me why—
    I hardly knew what it was like then.

        The doctor didn't know then
        so, he sent us to a special place:
        a Brigadoon in the twilight of
        skyscrapers and scraped skies.

The clouds whisked by
The traffic whittled by
The crowds grazed by
the twilight of motion—

nothing stood still but
who knew what was going on then.

       The audiologist did and
       so did the speech teacher.
       The doctor then reaffirmed.
       Still sleeping in the crib
       Still riding the carriage
       I sucked my thumb
           it was a thing to do.
               Nobody bothered
       to ask me why—
       I hardly knew what it was like then.

A hearing aid
    and an earmold:
the ultimate bandage for all the quiet
and the lack of not saying so.
       I hardly knew the difference then.

       What choices did I have
       while cuddly nestling
           in those reassuring
              cozy arms?

       That was who was I then
       who hardly had the preciosity then
     what differences they would make
now?

       Listen to this silence.

THE RALLY THAT STOOD
THE WORLD STILL

I stood wondering—among the excited crowd—
letting the world know the time had come—
if all the commotion would ever materialize.
Not that I had no confidence in the significance
of the intent—I'd just be fooling myself.

I just wondered if the world was more deaf than it
was willing to admit—would it be worth it at all?

I stood wondering—among the quiet hands
screaming at the world to be heard—
if all the shouting would be seen.
I was so numb with confusion
                    —the reality—

Two Deaf men and a hearing woman.
And there stood this other woman announcing
to the world— not that the lady won—
but that *deaf people are not ready to function in a hearing society.*
        Nor is she in the Deaf society.

I stood wondering—among the angry crowd—
whether the world might know the time has come—
If all the commotion was worth it at all. Indeed!
Indeed, for all the misanthropic wisdom
the hearing world had for deaf people, the demand
for a **Deaf President Now** was justified.
It was another *shot heard around the world.*

It was a time the world listened—
                    for a change!

BETWEEN CLASSES

Walking through the ball field,
    through noticing the green and muddy blends—
        footprints and packed grass
    scrambling from footprints of students scrambling
crossing to the other side of campus.

Hectic rush—
        when the bell rings
        my lecturing ceases—
            deadpanned smiling
            and chattering,
      slamming books,
        sleepyheads enlivening,
      heading for another class.
      a few slipping
        into jackets and gloves—
            either for the dorm
            or another class
        on the other side of campus

Passing time—
      scrambling through the fields beyond.
        classrooms are further away—
      on the other side of campus.

A CAMPUS STROLL AT GALLAUDET

Professorial enigma—
pithy academe
going off in tangents—
incongruous office and
campus politics
frequently
jar the intent.
I need to escape!
A stroll to regain.

A stroll—
an episodic walk—
a moment to recollect,
to recompose.
The linearity of things are
misaligned
momentarily,
periodically.

A stroll—
passing students,
colleagues,
and friends—
exchanging pleasantries,
catching up with campus news,
jokes to spare—
schmoozing along—
all for want to recapture
a lost moment.

Gone Far, Still Goin'

SAFE AND SOUND

In our sense of silence—
the noise.

An orchestration
of conundrum:
cumbrous movements,
an imminent
tempestuous
knell.

A vibration
for feeling
except
I haven't
the sophistication
to know
what or where
it is—
I take it
for granted
like a boom,
a bang,
a ding,
but not
a whimper.

Sound
a tutelage
for existence.

MY SENSE OF HEARING

There's no albatross
    To speak of
        Nor omens for spite—

                History states that
           We were sublimated
         For being oracular
      Because we were subversive
    With our semiotic hands—

    Speaking of which—
They never truly understood.

I've come to terms with reality
    I'm teaching them to understand
        Their eagerness to learn is immeasurable,

        I see.

        The truth of the matter is—
        They really don't know.

      We've affronted them for their imprudence
      We've chastised them for their ignorance
          And yet,
We've annihilated ourselves for our own impertinence
And left ourselves perpetually and bitterly embattled.

There's no albatross
    To speak of
        Nor omens for spite.

Gone Far, Still Goin'

TINNITUS

Loud.
      Louder than loud.
            Louder than louder.
       Loudest—
          a continuum.

Resonant turbulence
constantly ringing
contrapuntal gongs.

       I don't have my
       hearing aid on.

            Nodal pitches tingle
            the fugues of silence—

    louder,
       and louder,
           and louder,
              and louder.
Cranial sounds.

INSERTION

I.

Implosive sound
        from an irritating hearing aid
bypassing plains of
        the corrupted, the eroded—
            those deadened hairs
                in the cochlea—
                    the nautilus of the mind—
        acrimoniously tormented
            by the push of a megaphonic vibe
                spiraling through—
                    overpassing—
                            unheard of.

Acoustic highs—
        Raging plucks from the noises
leave them whispering
            tones
                            unheard of.

It's beyond incomprehensible.

    Take it off!
        What's the use?
            It's a dizzy tingling.

II.

Silence in the dark
    I lie motionless
            on a gurney
        until Meniere's ding
                awakens me groggily.

My head bandaged.
　　My mouth dry
　　　　begging for the mercy of an ice-cold drink
　　　　　　growling for a few saltines
　　　　　　　　struggling to stay awake
　　　　and struggling to fall back asleep.

　　Scampering nurses and a momentary surgeon
　　　　making the curtain calls—
　　　　　　checking for assurances

　　　　I hardly had the strength to applaud.

III.

A magnetizing button aside the auricle

　　none of that irritation inserted.
　　　　Sounds came through—
　　　　　　hardly a holler
　　　　　　　　but a roar
　　　　　　　　　　　　unheard of.

　　　　Squeaks and beeps
　　　　　　and Donald Duck
　　　　　　　　in every voice, too.

Sound—
　　a different
　　　　a strange
　　　　　　a new different
　　　　　　　　a new strange—
　　　　　　　　　　　a new set of acclimations.
　　Not like the hearing aid catching the rapping—
　　　　but waiting for knockdown resounding
　　　　　　　　of a repartee uninvited.

RHAPSODY

I'm drawn to song—
                watching operatic singers
                    rhapsodizing arias
                scaling intonations.

I'm drawn to music—
              via amplification
                by an induction coil—
                    I hear an intermezzo.

            I sway in the Virtuoso's dance
              animated by the sea of string bows
              and flittering, flickering fingers
                  swimming about the bridges,
                      climbing and rappelling
                  the shanks of horns,
          and climbing and rappelling
                      the stalks of reeds
                  at the oscillations
                  of the pandering baton.

I'm drawn to poetry—
              words orchestrating
              envisioned music.

Gone Far, Still Goin'

DEAF JEW

It's hard to know a Deaf Jew to share our own moments.
One doesn't hear *Shalom* often.
For me to email it or sign ILY—
it's the American way of saying the same thing
as long as I know who that Jewish Deaf person is.

It isn't even a culture to observe Shabbat among them.
One doesn't hear *Shabbat Shalom* or *Good Shabbos* so often.
For me, it's a quiet adoration and pride for her stance.
I cannot dignify her among those who know Israel
only by her scriptural significance.

Hearing people just don't seem to realize the magnitude
of the situation. We're too small to make a big deal—
but to most of us it's a hell of a deal to ignore. It angers us
that we cannot get the recognition we deserve to get. Damn, it
cost too much money for such a small project.

Jewish Deaf children just don't get a good Jewish education.
They learn from their Jewish Deaf parents who barely know
enough.
They learn from their Deaf friends who don't know the
difference.
Either they say I'm Jewish with ebullience or they say it with
utter indifference. No one seems to know for sure.

There have been so many tomorrows, but none ever came.
Yesterday didn't even pass. Today is still today. What is now?
Torah is living but the yad has gone beyond us. We've become
unreachable. We've become untouchable. We've become so
ignorant because we've wandered so far and yet we've reached
the sea.

SHOFAR

TEKIAH SHEVARIM-TERUAH TERUAH
TEKIAH SHEVARIM-TEKIAH
TEKIAH TERUAH TEKIAH-GEDOLAH

Speak to me, Elophim—
    I cannot hear You,
        or understand You
            Hebraically.
    I cannot see Your Hands.

Speak to me, Elohim—
      no man,
    whose hands I see
      is Your *dayyan*.
No rabbi—Your Word.

I am not free
    or enslaved—
        I cannot hear You.

Speak to me, Elohim—
    blare out Your *shofar*—
        I never could hear You,
          or see Your Hands.

Gone Far, Still Goin'

DEVOTION

Devotion
    to whom I hold
        deep in my heart
        heart of my soul—
        My loving wife and two
            adoring children.

Devotion—
    a collage of
        affection
        laughter
        anger
        forgiveness—
            the joy of belonging

Devotion—
    a mitzvah.

LYRICS I CAN'T FATHOM

Music is so loud.
All the kids are on the floor
in the roaring beat
mouthing the senseless
lyrics.

A dynamiting songfest
blasting from the floor
ratcheting beats
flagging the senseless
lyrics.

Countenance in the rhythm
tearing down faces
soaking soulful humping
rassling the senseless
lyrics.

I do see movements
gyrating beatific agitations
Beating! Beating!
Beating the senseless
lyrics.

The beauty of it all
is the crowding floor
holding them down
dancing the senseless
lyrics I can't fathom.

Gone Far, Still Goin'

THE JEWISH WEDDING IN THE GARDEN

Down the meadow
arranged flowers
lain on the idyllic path
between tall shady trees
beside small rustled shrubs
beneath the bridge
a rumbling stream—
chuppah.

MY SURNAME

My surname is not
    a Jewish name—
        not even a hint

My surname
    if not for the war
would still be Rabinowitz

Why give it away,
        they said.

What am I now?

YAHRZEIT
THE ANNIVERSARY

Candle Glass—
    Shabbat of Death—
a year passed—
    remember the dead.
A flame—
    Sukkot of Life—
        carry on.

Curtis Robbins

123

TERUMAH

Tell the Israelite people to bring Me gifts;
you shall accept gifts for Me from every
person whose heart so moves him.
                                    Exodus 25:2

My bar mitzvah
        at 24
                was certainly not like one
                        meant for one who's 13.

The Torah portion
        about Terumah—
                the tabernacle built
                        by one whose name
                                is my very own: Bezalel—
                                        in God's shadow.

For me
        the bar mitzvah
                was a confirmation
                of what I am—
                        a validation
                                of what is irrevocably true
                                        a mitzvah
                                                committed:
                        I am what I am.

Terumah!
        The rabbinic sages cast
        their shadows of doubt—
                        da'at of heresh demented
                        da'at of heresh demeaned
                        da'at of heresh deprecated—

the demonization of what I am—
the damning of my being
in God's shadow!

Heresh, Shoteh, v'Katan!
How could
I ask
if rabbis
presumed
I couldn't?

Heresh, Shoteh, v'Katan!

How could
Deaf Jews
give
if rabbis
presumed
they couldn't?

Heresh, Shoteh, v'Katan?

How can
rabbis
judge us
if they never
gave us
Torah?

FOR *DIE JUDEN*

For you
I will be a Dachau jew
and lie down in lime
with twisted limbs
and bloated pain
no mind can understand

"*The Genius*," *Leonard Cohen*

In a newsmagazine, I saw this
        picture of liberated
                        utterly dehydrated men
        in deathly torn stripes—
                brandished as *Jude*
        destined for the ungodly chambers
        for *die Juden.*

Their newfound freedom
                        as one can see
                is not one to forget or forgive
        surviving
Auschwitz, Treblinka, Dachau, and other camps
        as brandished souls
                        once
                        destined for the ungodly chambers
                                for *die Juden.*

Born at a time when all this happened,
                        I wonder—
                being deaf—
                        a timely,
                                manifested reminder?

Gone Far, Still Goin'

It may not be as blatant
as theirs,
but is a Deaf Jew as punishable
as the brandished *Jude*
destined for the ungodly chambers
for *die Juden*?

Heresh, Shoteh, v'Katan—
Am I chastised for this
for being Deaf
destined for the ungodly chambers
for *die Juden*?

A MESSAGE WRITTEN AND SNUGGLED BETWEEN THE CRACKS

A message written and snuggled
between the cracks at the Western Wall:

I ripped a piece of paper
something I found sufficed—
ripped from pamphlet where
there was enough space to write
a few words—a prayer for my
children and my wife.

A simple message of love and blessings
straightforward but short
to express my blessings to HaShem—
they are blessed and they are loved
and they cherished—
my children and my wife.

WHAT DOES SHABBAT MAKE?

Shabbat—
        the pillar of strength.

I'd welcome the Shabbat Queen
        but she'd be left in the cold.

Where do I rest?
        When do I feast?

My time.
        My place—
                my place
                in disarray.

I'd welcome the Shabbat Queen
        but she'd be left in the cold.

When do I *daven*?
        Where do I meditate?

My place.
        My time—
                my time
                out of sync.

I'd welcome the Shabbat Queen
        but she'd be left in the cold.

Shabbat—
        No one home.

Curtis Robbins

A PRAYER AT
THE WESTERN WALL

One year later
right after the '67 War
I walked through
one of the labyrinthine
tunnel-like corridors
of Old Jerusalem
leading to the Western Wall.

In its sandy disposition
absconding the Dome
divided by a partition
the mighty wall stood
withstanding messages stuffed
between quarried stones
chiseled in guarded prayers.

I stood in awe—
Hasidics davening
in their liturgical dancing
perpetuating
each word chanted
guarding precarious moments.

I was too fascinated to say a prayer.

Forty-one years later
I was walking through another
one of the labyrinthine
tunnel-like corridors
of Old Jerusalem
through the Jewish Quarter
leading to the Western Wall

Gone Far, Still Goin'

I stood in awe
a far cry from the last time:
granite floors, a partition,
railings, ramps, a museum,
and Israeli soldiers davening!
Hasidics still davening
in their ritual dancing—

I prayed.

I am a Deaf Jew
who cannot speak Hebrew
but in my own words
I could only speak
in awe of You—
accept me for what I am.

A MOMENT OF JOY

Darkness in the skies!
No clouds rolled by.
The sun has long gone.
Daisies couldn't thrive.

Makeshift bed boards
No furnace for the winter heat.
No ventilation for the summer breeze
Sufferings barely tended to.

The camo brethren have dispersed
Placed in barns fit for the farms.
The stench barely mattered.
Even the roof wasn't fit for home.

Hanukkah! Hanukkah?
Meals so unfit even for beasts!
The maccabees fought a battle
With just enough oil for light.

The dark, dank barn
And darkness in the sky.
A momentary dream—
A secret dark celebration!
A stolen potato?
An available candle?

ON THE VALIDITY OF PRAYER

Never again I will blame God for the lunacy of men.
Herman Taube

Man's piety—
   hide innate guilt
     for simply living—
  chaotic ambience—
    ambivalent
      wrong—
        ambiguity
          hidden in prayers

   begging God to rearrange
    the disarray
     of order—
        how wrongful
        how sinful
        how despicable
        how mutable
    beyond righteousness—
      beyond immeasurability
       of reality.

Prayers never answer
what Man himself cannot undo
what he had just impasssably done.

THE SILENT POET

You're reading me now!
I'm what's printed on this page.

   Wordflow comes from cams
    cams and gears
      coagulating
        thematic
          imaginations

  Whatever said
    that's irrevocably me.

    Poetry is an innocuous message—
      a movement of the moment!
    You are actually reading me
      through pulses
        and impulses.

        You are reading me
      through dreams
    and nightmares
   and spastic attacks
  of precocious
connotations.

You are reading me
  word bled
    from pen veins—
     a cleansing
       processed digitally.

The vocal voices
        with impugnable
            screams—
        the phones
                haven't stopped
                    ringing—
                            no turned heads ever.

        Urgent hands
                have been reaching
                        outwardly
                        looking for eyes—
                flagging the unfurled
                        was never
                        distracting enough.

        I wasn't meant to be liberated
                until you read me.

Gone Far, Still Goin'

ABOUT THE POET

Curtis Robbins, Ph.D., was born, raised, and educated in the vicinity of New York City. In 1963, he went to Gallaudet College (now University) in Washington, D.C., and acquired sign language there. He then earned a master's degree from New York University, and worked as a vocational rehabilitation counselor for two years. He later obtained a doctorate in education technology from University of Maryland, and his career includes several professorial positions at Gallaudet University, American University, and George Washington University. In 2018, Curtis and his wife relocated from Maryland to Florida.

Curtis began writing poetry at the tender age of 14. *In Spite of Everything* was his first book in 2015, and he has had his works published in numerous other publications and books. To learn more about Curtis and his work, visit www.curtdeafpoet.com.

www.ingramcontent.com/pod-product-compliance
Lightning Source LLC
Chambersburg PA
CBHW072153090426
42740CB00012B/2253